INTRODUCTION by Natalie Weinstein

The cave woman turned to the cave man and said, "Honey, I can't live like this a minute longer. We've got to clean up this place and get some new skins and cave paintings."

That's where it all began and will continue until the end of human existence. People need to "decorate". It fulfills a basic nesting instinct and satisfies the artistic yearnings deep inside all of us. People want to decorate for themselves, their families, their friends. Some people even like to decorate. They either become interior designers, have a serious need to torture themselves, or are people like you and me who read and write books about interior design.

This book, written after decades as an interior designer, teacher and lecturer, is meant to help that person who likes, wants and needs to decorate. It can be read in one sitting and its purpose is to give a common sense overview of the interior designer's craft to those who have little time in their busy schedule to read about it, and even less time to do it.

For me, I love to decorate. I have been doing it since I was five and probably will go to my grave with a floor plan in one hand and fabric swatches in the other. Decorating has enabled me to meet some wonderfully interesting people, play out my fantasies in other people's homes and offices, and stimulate me to keep thinking creatively every day of my life.

Being challenged to answer design questions or solving problems has been great fun. It's like successfully putting the pieces of a puzzle together. And how often the same questions are asked! This book was inspired by those questions, as I have been inspired by those questioners.

The photographs in this book are all of room designs that I have created in the hopes of fulfilling my clients' individual wants and needs. They are artfully captured on film by the talented Jack Ader.

So let us continue to explore the exciting world of interior design. Perhaps some day, our paths will cross in that elusive and wonderful pursuit of the beautifully decorated space.

The Hundred Most Often Asked Interior Design Questions

by

Natalie Weinstein, ALLIED ASID

Photography and Design

By

Jack Ader

© 2006 - Natalie Weinstein Design Associates
Published by Images for Presentation
First Edition
ISBN - 0-9749531-1-3

Dedicated to my mother and father,
Hilda and Joseph London,
who were the first to decorate my life
with beauty and love

Table of Contents

Chapter I Floor Plans & Furniture Arrangement 13

Chapter II Art History & Furniture Styles 21

Chapter III Color 27

Chapter IV Fabrics, Upholstery & Window Treatments 33

Chapter V Walls & Wall Coverings 41

Chapter VI Floor Coverings 49

Chapter VII Lighting 57

Chapter VIII Wood & Wood Furniture 63

Chapter IX Art & Accessories 69

Chapter X Decorating With a Budget 75

Chapter XI Working with an Interior Designer 79

Questions

Chapter I: Floor Plans and Furniture Arrangement

1. What is a floor plan and how does it help?

2. Why is it so important to make an accurate floor plan?

3. How do you know what to put on the floor plan?

4. Are there tools to help make a floor plan?

5. Is there a trick to using the templates for a beginner?

6. How does a floor plan help you decide what style of furniture you want?

7. How can a floor plan help if you're not sure whether the house you have lived in for years is where you want to remain?

8. What is "multi-functional" space?

9. Where do designers find "hidden" spaces in a house?

10. How are the lifestyles of the 21st century affecting space planning?

11. What about kid's rooms?

12. What about moving to a smaller space?

13. What does common sense have to do with floor plans?

Chapter II: Art History and Furniture Styles

14. Who was the first interior designer?

15. Where was the first furniture seen?

16. Where did the architectural designs of today originate?

17.   Weren't the Romans credited with the designs of early furniture and architecture?

18.   Why don't we hear much about furniture styles after the fall of the Roman Empire?

19.   What was the Renaissance?

20.   What is the difference between a furniture "period" and "style"?

21.   What kind of furniture styles do we use today?

22.   How do I know which styles there are, what they look like and how to put them together?

23.   How can I create an eclectic look?

Chapter III: Color

24.   How does color affect your room?

25.   With so many colors to choose from, what do I have to know about color to use it properly when decorating?

26.   What is tonal value and chromatic intensity?

27.   What are the differences between a complimentary color scheme, a related color scheme and a monochromatic color scheme?

28.   How do you choose a color scheme and what do you start with?

29.   How does color create unity?

30.   Do different furniture styles dictate different color schemes?

31.   How do you create a "new look" with color?

Chapter IV: Fabrics, Upholstery & Window Treatments

32.   How do natural and synthetic fabrics differ?

33.   What types of finishes are available on fabrics?

34.   How does the weave of a fabric affect its use?

35.   How does texture differ from pattern?

36.   What kinds of fabrics go with formal and informal styles?

37.   When shopping in a retail store, how do you choose the best fabric for the pieces of furniture you select?

38.   What does an upholstery workroom do?

39.   How do you know how much fabric you will need?

40.   What about fabric coordination? How do I get that designer look?

41.   What window treatments are "in", and what kinds go with what style?

Chapter V: Walls and Wall Coverings

42.   How do walls function in my design plan?

43.   What about defects such as obstructions, jogs and boxed-out areas?

44.   What types of wall applications do I have to choose from?

45.   What architectural features are used on walls?

46.   What options do I have in choosing wallpaper?

47.   How do I know how much wallpaper to buy?

48. What options do I have with paint?

49. What effect does fabric have on walls?

50. What effect does wood have on walls?

51. What other products are used on walls?

Chapter VI: Floor Covering

52. What kinds of floor coverings are available to choose from and how do you determine what to use where?

53. What should I know about choices for wall-to-wall carpet?

54. How is carpet measured?

55. What should I know about oriental rugs, types, coordination, size and color?

56. What about creating designer looks using area rugs and wall-to-wall carpeting?

57. When should you consider wood floors?

58. When and where are ceramic, porcelain and other hard surface floors a consideration?

59. Is vinyl a good choice today?

60. What about granite and marble?

Chapter VII: Lighting

61. Why is lighting so important?

62. What kinds of lighting choices are there?

63. When is recessed lighting used?

64. Are ceiling fixtures "in"?

65. How do lamps and sconces enhance the lighting in a room?

66. What other lighting effects are there?

67. What about watts and bulbs?

68. What about halogen?

69. Is neon an option in residences?

70. What is a lighting plan?

Chapter VIII: Woods and Wood Furniture

71. What's the difference between wood furniture and micas?

72. Is a veneer not as good as solid wood?

73. What kinds of woods are popular today with the general public?

74. How does the type of wood affect the style of furniture?

75. How does the color of the wood affect the décor?

76. When would you use a custom cabinet shop?

77. When dealing with a woodworking shop, how do you know you will get what you ordered?

78. How important is the cabinet construction to you?

79. What about refinishing existing wood furniture?

80. How do you maintain fine wood furniture?

Chapter IX: Art and Accessories

81. What do accessories do for a room?

82. Why is it difficult for most people to accessorize?

83.   What are functional accessories?

84.   What are decorative accessories?

85.   What are collectibles?

86.   What is considered "art"?

87.   How do you know how high to hang pictures?

88.   What about plants?

89.   How do you begin to accessorize?

90.   How do you learn to accessorize like the professionals?

Chapter X: Decorating with a Budget

91.   Why is it necessary to have a decorating budget?

92.   How do you know which are important budget items for you?

93.   How do you set up a budget?

94.   When is spending more smarter?

95.   What do you do if you have very little resources?

Chapter XI: Working with an Interior Designer

96.   What is the function of an interior designer?

97.   How do interior designers work and how can they save you money?

98.   Do you give up control and relinquish your right to choose what you want when you work with an interior designer?

99.   What should you expect from your interior designer?

100.   What should your interior designer expect from you?

Chapter I

Floor Plans and Furniture Arrangement

1. What is a floor plan and how does it help?

A floor plan is a road map of a room drawn as if you were looking down from the rafters. It shows the length and width of the floor space, as well as locations of doors, openings, windows, fireplaces and heating. It is drawn to scale like a road map and the key will tell you in what scale it is drawn. Most residential floor plans are in 1/4" scale (meaning 1/4" = 1'), and most commercial plans are 1/8" scale (1/8" = 1'). If you get a plan from a brochure or newspaper, look for words that say "dimensions approximate" to know whether you have an accurate floor plan on which to place your furniture or you need to field measure or get an architect's plan. Measuring your room with an adequate tape measure (not a 12" ruler or your big feet!) is a must before you go shopping for furniture. Even if you have existing furniture, it's a lot easier on your back to measure the pieces and move them on paper.

2. Why is it so important to make an accurate floor plan?

Measuring your furniture and dimensioning it on paper forces you to visualize the space as it will be before you actually move the furniture you have or buy new pieces. This affords you the opportunity to change your mind if it doesn't look well before you make a costly mistake or start down a wrong path. Invariably, one mistake leads to others in an attempt to repair the first.

Remember - if it doesn't look right on the plan, it won't look any better in the room.

3.How do you know what to put on the floor plan?

The way to determine what to put on your floor plan is to make a list. List first the pieces of furniture you truly need in the room, as well as those existing pieces which will stay. Analyze the space, not as it has always been, but according to your lifestyle now. Realize that certain pieces of furniture can function for more than one use (i.e., a built-in wall cabinet, bookcase, bar, storage, audio center, etc.), giving you additional space in a room for other things. When you have completed your "needs" list, make a "wish" list. Think about all the things you would love to have but that aren't essential. Perhaps you will be able to incorporate some of these items in your current redecorating project. You may discover that a piano or a home theatre is not so far fetched. Go for it - if space and budget will allow.

4. Are there tools to help make a floor plan?

Many art supply stores carry graph paper (make sure you check the scale) and furniture templates (also scaled correctly to your needs). You'd do best with 1/4". These templates are like the stencils we played with when we were kids. Just trace around their outlines on the graph paper and you will see how the furniture you desire fits in the room. The problem with templates is that you are tempted to use exclusively the sizes and shapes of what they show. They are meant to be helpful. But once you get the idea of scale, you can make your own outline of something you already have or have seen that you would like to include in your room, making sure your measurements are accurate.

5. Is there a trick to using the templates for a beginner?

For beginners, put the traced outlines on a blank piece of paper and cut them out. Then you can move the furniture pieces around on your graph paper to see how they fit in different room locations. It's easier than moving the real thing, and gives you all your options without committing to one space or wearing a hole in the paper with your eraser.

6. How does a floor plan help you decide what style of furniture you want?

It doesn't. A floor plan just shows you the space it will take up. It won't show you if it's French Provincial or American Federal. However, if a floor plan has a real sense of balance (symmetry) with a sofa in the center of an arrangement and a pair of chairs and tables on either side, there is a strong likelihood that the the room is more traditional. Asymmetrical floor plans with modular or angular sofas are a clue to more contemporary styles.

7. How can a floor plan help if you're not sure that the house you have lived in for years is where you want to remain?

Many people today opt to renovate and redecorate, rather than relocate. There are many reasons for this. They like the neighborhood and school district. It's convenient for work. It's a hassle and expensive to move. Taxes would be higher in a new home. They would actually have to pack all they've accumulated for the last ten years! It's a frustrating and annoying process to sell your home, and even more difficult to find a home that's perfect for your needs which won't have to be renovated as well.

So what's the solution? First, look at your existing home with a different perspective. Ask yourself if you would like to remain were the rooms used differently, or combined, if the kitchen and bathrooms were redone, if more closets and storage could be created.

If the layout of such major changes are beyond you, it may be prudent to call in a designer or architect to do a study. For a consultation fee, you may discover that it is more cost effective to renovate than move, and the changes may give you all the things you really want.

8. What is "multi-functional" space?

When designers use the term "multi-functional", they simply mean that a space is too valuable to be used for only one purpose. For example, a home where kids are grown and off to college or married may have 2-3 unused bedrooms. Because these rooms act as guest bedrooms a few times a year doesn't mean they can't function with an additional purpose as well. One certainly can remain with a full bedroom set, but the others could have a sleep sofa, "Murphy" bed (bed unit built into the wall) or trundle bed (pull-out bed under another bed). Now they can become an exercise room, sewing room, library or second den, as well.

Perhaps a small bedroom directly behind the master can be opened up with pocket doors to enlarge the master bedroom by creating a "sitting room" most of the year, adding more closet space. By locking the doors, it can then be easily returned to guest space for the few times it is needed for visitors.

9. Where do designers find "hidden" spaces in a house?

When redesigning space, designers don't leave anything out. Basements, attics, and garages all come into play because they know it is more cost effective to utilize what's already there than to plan new construction to enlarge the existing space. Designers can carve larger spaces from smaller ones to fill more functional needs. For example, a larger kitchen can be created by using the existing kitchen and dinette, and a small porch or guest room adjacent to it can be a new dining space. Another option is opening the den to kitchen and eating space, creating a great room.

A few years back, dining rooms were starting to become obsolete, but today many people are cooking and entertaining at home and want a larger space for dining. Sometimes it is a space flip-flopped with the living room. The trick is to look at a space, not as it is, but as it could be.

10. How are the lifestyles of the 21st century affecting space planning?

More and more people today, because of their busy and hectic lifestyles view their residences as a refuge, a place to come home to and enjoy. People are now looking to their homes to fill the needs of a "mini-vacation" because time does not allow for too many of the real ones. Instead of going out, people are looking forward to staying in.

Why not? Picture this. You've come home from a long and frustrating day at work, and so has your spouse. You need to relax and unwind, release some of the negative energy that's been building. So you get on the treadmill in your exercise room as you pop some dinner in the oven and you start to feel a little better. Next, you turn on the whirlpool in your "tub for two" and the cares of the day seem to float away. By the time dinner is done, you feel almost human, and are ready to curl up with another warm body (if no spouse is available, you may have to settle for the dog) and pop a video on the big screen. Before you know it, life isn't so bad.

Perhaps this is not your scenario even though you'd love it to be. Somehow car pools, homework, and the telephone get in the way. But you can see how and why the lifestyles of today are creating new design plans for your home. It's become O.K. to indulge in creature comforts and share them with family and friends as well. It's almost become a necessity.

11. What about kids rooms?

Designers are good - but they are not magicians!

For most parents, the answer is CLOSE THE DOOR. But ask yourself the common sense questions of space planning and see if you've met their needs in the furniture you've provided. Is there adequate closet and drawer space? Is there a place for computer, school and library books, desk surfaces for homework? Is there wall space for posters and collectibles (of their choice, not yours)? Is there room for a friend to sleep over or just visit? Have you shown them care in planning and purchasing their furniture? Was it their choice, too?

If the room is for little children, have you provided adequate storage to put toys away and placed hooks and hangers at their height? Have you helped them develop pride in their space and how to take care of it and clean up? Have you praised them enough and taught them respect for their things? Have you made them part of the decision process on their level?

If the answer to all these questions is "yes" and there's still a mess, you can always CLOSE THE DOOR!

Hint: Kids' rooms can be a "do it yourself" family project. It's fun, cost effective and it works.

12. What about moving to a smaller space?

When the time is right or necessary to move and the space is smaller, (i.e. from a large house to a condo, or to an apartment) judicious space planning is essential. The basic floor plan should first be determined with a list of the things that are "musts" to take. The hardest thing for people to do is part with treasures that have been collected over the years. But making a warehouse of your new home isn't exactly ideal either.

So, clean up, throw out, and give away (especially clothes you haven't worn for years) and bring in the closet-organizing people! Then sit down with your floor plan and try to incorporate the things you love best. Chances are this move is traumatic as well as exciting, and planning is the key to sanity.

Start with the basics, but view them honestly in the new space. If a piece of furniture doesn't work or is creating a problem for other existing furnishings, you might consider giving it to a family member, rather than selling or donating it. Then think about reupholstery or a new carpet or wall color to give everything a fresh look. Maybe a new "you" has emerged since you last furnished and you want to add pieces or accessories to what you have reflecting this.

Take your floor plan with you so you can marry the old with the new in a pleasing way. Then you can enjoy the process of shopping for new things without the fear of making a mistake.

13. What does common sense have to do with floor plans?

Everything!

Ask yourself:

Would you put all tall pieces on one side of a room?

Would you put all furniture in the middle of a room or against the walls?

Would you put the furniture so close together that you'd have to pole vault over something to get into the seating area?

Would you put tables so far away from sofas and chairs that you couldn't reach them?

Would you have only one seating area in a large room, or three to four in a small room?

Sounds silly- right? Not really. People think that when they are decorating, "creativity" supercedes common sense. Well, think again.

Analyze any room you like in a magazine and you will see that designers start with these basic parameters and then do their magic with color, fabric, floors, walls, windows, lighting and accessories.

QUESTIONS TO ASK YOURSELF OR DISCUSS WITH YOUR DESIGNER TO GET THE MOST USE AND ENJOYMENT FROM YOUR HOME

1.   What are my current needs?

2.   What are my short-term and long-term needs?

3.   How can I incorporate more than one function in certain spaces?

4.   Will construction or renovation create a better space plan?

5.   How will modernizing the kitchen and baths give me more space?

6.   How can basements, attics, laundry rooms, garages and outside porches help add living and working space to my home?

7.   How can the furniture I select give me an added feeling of well-used space?

8.   How can existing closets and other storage areas be made more functional?

Chapter II

Art History and Furniture Styles: Where it All Began

14. Who was the first interior designer?

Prehistoric man was the first interior designer, decorating caves with wall paintings and animal skins, as well as designing utensils and creating statuary. All were symbolic of successful harvests, hunts, great events and procreation. They also fulfilled a sense of bonding with nature. These early homes satisfied the nesting instinct inherent in many species, especially humans.

15. Where was the first furniture seen?

Ancient Egyptian tombs reveal the stool with it's animal-shaped legs as the early forerunner of the chair. Animal legs on many pieces of furniture throughout the centuries take their roots from this early period. "X" shaped benches, also popular then, are used today for pull-up seating and under vanities and parsons tables. The bed or bed stand, another early piece of furniture, functioned for relaxing, as well as sleeping.

16. Where did the architectural designs of today originate?

The Greeks of antiquity, who prided themselves in searching for perfection in all things, created the architectural moldings and designs on buildings and furniture that are still used today. But their inspiration dated back past the Egyptian columns to the ancient monolithic structures called Stonehenge.

17. Weren't the Romans credited with the design of early furniture and architecture?

The Romans were conquerors of foreign lands and foreign styles. They modified the various styles of civilizations they conquered, but were not great originators. Through their adaptation, the Egyptian, Greek, Spanish and Turkish styles were perpetuated. The Greek klismos chair was one such style carried through to today, as well as bed and table designs in marble and wood painted finishes. Glassware and polished bronze and silver mirrors, however, were perfected by the Romans.

18. Why don't we hear much about furniture styles after the fall of the Roman Empire?

For several hundred years, culture and civilization declined until the Gothic Church styles of the 13th century brought back simple pieces of furniture such as stools, benches and chests. The ornately carved clergy seats led to the more elaborate furniture to come.

19. What was the Renaissance?

The word literally means "rebirth" - a re-awakening, specifically, of the culture and the art forms of Greece and Rome. Starting in Italy and spreading to France, England, Spain and Holland, this classical re-awakening was the forerunner of most of our furniture and architectural styles today.

20.What is the difference between a furniture "period" and "style"?

A furniture period is usually attributed to the reigning monarch of a country, sometimes because he or she was responsible for it, but not necessarily. For example, Louis XIV of France was directly involved in the art and architecture that carries his name, whereas Queen Anne of England was not. A furniture "style" is usually associated with it's specific designer, such as England's Thomas Chippendale or America's Duncan Phyfe.

21. What kind of furniture styles do we use today?

Furniture styles today can be broadly described as traditional, provincial, contemporary, modern and eclectic. Traditional describes the styles of the 17th, 18th, and 19th centuries, as in France and England. They are popular because they are timeless, never going in or out of style. They can be authentic antiques, reproductions or modifications.

Provincial, literally meaning "of the provinces", and colonial, meaning "of the colonies", are simplified court styles using available local woods. Because the furniture is more comfortable and less formal, it gained popularity with the "common people".

Contemporary furniture takes the traditional styles of the past and translates them into today's needs, keeping the flavor but not necessarily the style itself. It's lines are generally straighter and much less ornamental. Modern furniture attempts to use present-day materials to create a new and functional furniture style.

Eclectic is a combination of furniture styles. When done well, it can create a harmonious blend of individualistic taste. When not, it can be a disaster!

22. How can I create an eclectic look?

The blend is what's most important. Ask yourself if the pieces have the same degree of formality, proportion and feel. Check magazines and showrooms to see how the experts do it. Avoid using more than three or more styles in one room.

23. How do I know which styles there are, when they occurred and where?

The chart on the following pages will help you see which styles occurred, when and where.

GUIDE TO FURNITURE PERIODS

This brief reference guide to furniture periods will help you see what was happening where in terms of furniture styles. The dates of some periods or styles overlap. For this reason, consider the given dates as approximate. These dates simply serve to help you fix periods and styles in their correct century and sequence, and to see the relationship between the development of furniture styles in different countries.

	FRANCE	ENGLAND	AMERICA	OTHER COUNTRIES
Early Times				Classic in: Egypt 4500 BC-640 AD Greece 2000 BC-30 AD Rome 753 BC-400 AD
Middle Ages (1100 AD-1500 AD)	Gothic	Gothic		Gothic in Italy and Spain
16th Century	Renaissance	Renaissance Tudor 1500 - 1558		Renaissance in Italy, Spain, and Holland

(24)

KING-TISDELL COTTAGE
514 East Huntington Street
Savannah, Georgia

Dedicated to the preservation of *Black History and Culture.* The museum contains art objects, documents, personal articles and furnishings particular to a coastal Afro-American home (circa 1890). *Open daily.*

Photo by Jim McElholm

Dixie Postcards & Souvenir Sales, Savannah, Georgia 31405
Tel. (912) 234-2300

SPACE RESERVED FOR U.S. POSTAL SERVICE

POST CARD

0 32719 20046 4

17th Century	Louis XIV 1643 - 1715	Jacobean 1603 - 1648 William and Mary 1689 - 1702	Early American 1607 - 1725	Late Renaissance in Italy, Spain, and Holland
18th Century	Early French Provincial 1650 - 1800 Louis XV 1715 - 1774 Louis XVI 1774 - 1789 Directoire 1795 - 1804	Queen Anne 1702 - 1714 Georgian 1714 - 1820 Chippendale 1718 - 1779 Adam 1728 - 1792 Hepplewhite unknown - 1786 Sheraton 1715 - 1806	Colonial 1725 - 1780	
19th Century	Empire 1804 - 1815 Art Nouveau 1890 - 1905	Regency 1810 - 1820 Victorian 1837 - 1901	Duncan Phyfe 1768 - 1854 Federal 1790 - 1830 American Victorian 1840 - 1880 Shaker 1776 - 1860	Biedermeier in Germany 1815 - 1860
20th Century	Modern	Modern	Modern	Danish Modern in Sweden, Denmark and Finland

(25)

Helpful Furniture Terms to Know:

Armoire	Tall French clothes wardrobe, used today for TV, computer, crafts and bar storage, as well
Bergère	All-upholstered armchair
Bombé	A swelling curve to the front of a piece of furniture, giving the chest its name
Cabriole	Carved animal leg
Chaise	Original meaning (in French) for a side chair, often used today to mean chaise lounge or one-piece unit that looks like a chair with attached ottoman
Commode	Low chest of drawers
Etagère	Hanging or standing open shelves
Marquetry	Inlay of woods
Neo classic	Style referring to a revival of the Greek and Roman style with a new interpretation
Ormulu	Gilded bronze, usually as ornamentation or handles (popular in Louis XV style furniture).
Stretchers	Leg connectors on chairs and tables, often seen on early English and American furniture styles
Semanier	Narrow seven drawer dresser

Chapter III

Color

24. How does color affect your room?

Color is probably the most important and change-pro-moting design element people have to work with. Color can make a room appear larger or smaller, warm or cool, cheery or subdued. It can add drama to an ordinary space or unify an area with many diverse elements. It's the least costly way to make the greatest change in a room. Color, however, must be under-stood and carefully controlled.

25. With so many colors to choose from, what do I have to know about color to use it properly when decorating ?

You should know that our color parameters come from a color theory based on light passing through a prism, creating the colors of a rainbow. These colors are called spectrum colors and when formed into a circle become a color wheel.

3 primary colors: red, blue and yellow

3 secondary colors: purple, green and orange (each made up of two primaries in equal proportion, i.e. red + blue = purple, yellow + blue = green, and red + yellow = orange)

12 tertiary (a combination of a primary and a secondary color)

12 quaternary (a combination of a tertiary with its sec-ondary or primary) and hundreds and hundreds of color combi-nations from these.

The name of a color is called its hue. And that's just the beginning!

26. What is tonal value and chromatic intensity?

Value, tonal value, or tone are all terms that relate to the degree of lightness or darkness of a color. These are made by adding varying amounts of white or black. When we use the word "tint" (the lighter degrees of a color) or "shade" (the darker degrees of a color), we are describing tonal value. There are literally hundreds of tints or shades that can be created.

Intensity, chromatic intensity, or chroma are words that describe the degree of brightness or dullness of a color. The pure color (nothing added to it) is considered the most intense. To make it duller, we add its compliment (the color opposite it on the color wheel), and by using larger amounts of this compliment, we can dull it down to a color so neutral it becomes gray or dull brown.

27. What is the difference between a "related color scheme" and a "monochromatic color scheme"?

Colors that are opposite one another on the color wheel are considered complimentary (i.e. yellow's compliment is purple, blue's compliment is orange, red's compliment is green). Complimentary color schemes create contrast. Usually they create bright and cheery room settings when they are more intense. Most people, however, cannot live in surroundings for too long that are very intense. So generally, most areas are dulled down to some degree, leaving the more intense colors for accents.

Related color schemes are those which start from the same color base (i.e. blue, blue-green and green). On the color wheel, they are next to each other and end when a new primary color begins, creating a new color base. When using these colors together, as with a complimentary color scheme, varying the intensity is most important.

A monochromatic color scheme is one in which the values (light and dark tones) of the same color are used together (varying shades of blue and green from sea foam to teal is one example). Many people relate best to this color scheme because it produces a calming result and is probably the easiest to achieve. Designers often use it and add interest through differing textures and "tone on tone" patterns in the same color family, varying the intensity.

28. How do you choose a color scheme and what do you start with?

Choosing a color scheme isn't easy. There are many varying factors. Since it has been proven that people relate emotionally to color (evidenced in school rooms and work places, hospitals and prisons) and we've always described feelings in color, ("in the pink", "feeling blue", "green with envy"), we must recognize that different colors make us feel differently when we are surrounded by them. Their intensity and value affect us, as well.

In addition, people are affected by colors that are "in". Color preferences have always been cyclical, (earth tones, neutrals, pastels, jewel tones) generally set forth by the design industry to create change so people will want to redecorate. The availability and presentation of certain colors over others set this trend.

But decorating according to what is "in", which might soon be "out", can prove to be expensive and time consuming. So choose colors which you will want to have around you for a long time. Think carefully about how you want to feel when you come home. If your work life is stressful, do you want to come home to a dramatic environment or one that is calming and restful? If your conservative work image is not the "real" you, do you want to feel enervated or introduce more drama with the color palette of your home?

So, while it is true that color availability changes with the market trends, color should be a personal choice. Whether you choose cool colors (blues, greens and purples) which have a receding effect, warm colors (reds and oranges), or bright colors (yellows), which have a bolder and larger effect, neutrals, or a combination of these, make sure you want to live with them for the long haul. Remember, most people won't redecorate for at least ten years, despite what they may plan when purchasing.

Start with one element that strikes your fancy. Sometimes it is a beautiful fabric or wall covering. Other times, it's a wonderful area rug. It might even be a treasured piece of art work or collectible. Often, colors are drawn from the natural elements outside of the home (desert, ocean, mountains, etc.). The color or colors drawn from these can set the scheme for not only one room, but invariably spread to connecting spaces as well.

29. How does color create unity?

Color creates unity better than any other design element. In effect, it brings together every design element from differing furniture styles to diverse fabric textures. It even plays down poor architectural features and enhances good ones by blending them in, or highlighting them with the same or different colors.

Color can create unity and flow between several rooms by weaving the same threads of color throughout. This need not be boring, if there is enough diversity in pattern, texture and color focus. For example, an accent color in one room can take center stage in another.

Most homes today have entries, living rooms, dining rooms, kitchens and dens visible to one another. The color unity throughout these spaces is not only good design, but psychologically more comfortable to live with.

30.Do different furniture styles dictate different color schemes?

Period styles, when used in their day, were associated with certain color schemes (Louis XIV, jewel tones; Louis XV, pastels; etc.). Other than in museums, most people who live with traditional or period styles get the effect with furniture and fabric more so than with color. Traditional patterns in rugs and fabrics are available in so many colorways. Today, most people take advantage of the choices to blend with their own personal taste.

31. How do you create a "new look" with color?

When the budget is low, when time is running out, or when your furniture is still in good shape but you can't look at your room a minute longer, get out the paint samples! Changing the color of your walls and/or bringing in new color accents through pillows, art accessories, flowers, etc. will revitalize your old furnishings in a way which can be truly amazing, especially if your room began with a basically neutral palette.

Neutral may be "safe", but can tend to become boring if you don't watch out. So "live a little" by bringing in color with things that are not too expensive and can be changed easily, such as accessories, art and wall color.

Chapter IV

Fabrics, Upholstery and Window Treatments

32. How do natural and synthetic fabrics differ?

Natural fabrics made from animal or vegetable sources such as wool, silk, linen and cotton, while more elegant, tend to be more costly and have certain disadvantages such as pilling (wool), wrinkling (linen), fading (cotton), and not standing up to heavy use or sunlight (silk). When specified properly according to function, they allow many years of quality wearability using the real thing.

Synthetics, made from chemicals, attempt to eliminate the disadvantages of natural fibers while duplicating the look. Some are nylon, polyester, olefin, rayon and acetate. They have been perfected today to wear well, look well, and are generally more "budget friendly". Always look at the fiber content when purchasing fabric to help you decide what fabrics should be used where.

33. What types of finishes are available on fabrics?

Soil and fire retardants, water resisters and vinylizing finishes are available on many fabrics today. They often go under different company names, but mean the same thing. For example, Scotchguard, Zepel and Teflon are some of the soil-resisting finishes. These are applied at the mill and tend to hold up better than those sprayed on in the home. They can, after time, begin wear off, so using an applied finish later on can maintain the soil resistance of the fabric.

Water-resistant finishes would be an advantage in bathrooms, porches, boats or wherever water or mildew is a problem, or select fabrics used for outdoor awnings or furniture to begin with.

The law requires fabrics to go through a flame-retardant process. Always check the label, however, especially if it is an unusual fabric, or if it's for a commercial use and will require a specific flame rating.

Vinylizing in a matte or shiny form, is a process which applies a vinyl protective coating to many fabrics, allowing it to be washable and scrubbable. It can be used for kitchen chair seats, bar stools and parsons tables. Fabric houses can supply these finishes upon request at an additional cost per yard, or there are companies that specialize in its application. This is done when fabric is still on the bolt.

34. How does the weave of a fabric affect its use?

All woven fabrics are made up of warps and wefts. The pattern they make (the weave) affects its durability, as well as its look. A plain weave (warp and wefts yarn over and under each other) is used to create fabrics such as broadcloths, muslin and taffeta. A basket weave is a variation of this. Their flat surfaces can show soil. Twill heirloom weaves (diagonal ribs) in fabrics such as denim and flannel are more soil and wrinkle resistant. Satin weaves used in satin and damask (a weave that appears to have threads running only one way) can be strong, depending on the fabrics used. Pile weaves (threads pulled to have a looped surface) can be cut (velvet, velour) or uncut (terry cloth). They can be luxurious and durable.

35. How does texture differ from pattern?

The texture of a fabric (smooth or rough, thick or thin, how loosely or tightly it is woven) has an effect both visually as well as to the touch. The texture of certain fabrics today can be equally as important as the pattern. For example, ultra-suede, vinyl and leather, which may or may not have a pattern or embossing, have a certain feel and are used well in certain contemporary or eclectic settings.

Some wonderful room designs have hardly any pattern at all. They are made interesting and effective by combining many textures (i.e. leather, suede, metal, glass, etc.).

36. What kinds of fabrics go with formal and informal styles?

Velvets, brocades, damask, crewel, tapestries, silks, satins and taffetas are considered more formal fabrics and go with traditional styles. Chintzes, toile de jouys, and linens can be both formal (Louis XVI) and informal (Country or French Provincial). Cottons such as corduroy, denim, sail cloth, wool and many synthetics are mainly used for more informal and contemporary styles. Sometimes there is a carry over, but it must be carefully done, so that an eclectic feeling is created.

37. When shopping in a retail store, how do you choose the best fabric for the pieces of furniture you select?

Most stores have fabric swatches from the manufacturer. If they are organized at all, it is usually by color, not by pattern or style. You must take into consideration all the fabrics you wish to select for your room setting, the sizes of the upholstered pieces and the window treatments-in effect, everywhere that fabrics will be used.

Don't be afraid to select more than one patterned material. The old days of one solid, one stripe and one print are long gone. Be cognizant, however, of the proportion or scale of the patterns, as well as the colors. If you are making selections from more than one furniture store, ask for swatches or samples to take with you. Make sure they are large enough to work with. Remember, color blend alone won't do it. Patterns have to be pleasing together and proportionate as well. Using solids on large pieces will create a different effect than a plaid, stripe or floral. Think about the total room when choosing what goes where.

Wall covering and flooring must be considered as well. A patterned area rug will dictate different fabric placement than a solid wall-to-wall carpet, for example.

38. What does an upholstery workroom do?

Many designers prefer custom upholstery workrooms to purchasing ready-made furniture for their clients because of versatility and quality control. The upholsterer makes or uses custom furniture frames, so choice of size and style is endless, bound only by the limits of imagination (and hopefully, good taste).

Often times, custom draperies are also made in an upholstery workroom, as well as re-upholstering of existing furniture (sofas, chairs, benches, etc.). This provides a more "one stop shopping" experience. The upholsterer usually provides selections of materials from fabric books like designers use, or he or she may send you to mill converters like Kravet Fabrics, Robert Allen and Duralee, where you could not purchase directly on our own.

Generally, the labor cost of the upholstery is separate from the fabric charge to upholster, and it may cost more than a furniture company which manufactures and sells standard size selections in large quantity. But, if quality and custom sizing is important, this route might be your preference and may be more cost effective in the long run.

39. How do you know how much fabric you will need?

If you shop retail, they will automatically specify the amount of fabric you will need for pieces you order from them. They will check your fabric selections for width and repeat and list it on your bill with the grade of fabric to determine the total price you will pay. An upholstery workroom will specify in the same way, providing yardage for window treatments, upholstered walls, or reupholstery needs.

If you are shopping for fabric on your own, check width and repeat and order a little extra in case of a mishap or for accessories, pillows, etc. Later on, you may not get the same dye lot or the fabric may be discontinued.

40. What about fabric coordination? How do I get that designer look?

Designers are people who are immersed in fabrics, furniture, and wall coverings day in and day out. We weren't born with this knowledge. We learn it and live it daily. If you are interested and have the time, broaden your horizons, develop your taste and widen your choices by looking in decorating magazines like Architectural Digest, House and Garden, Interiors, etc. Also, go to fine furniture stores and study the room settings, visit designer showcases when available, as well as museums which show period furniture rooms. If you are by nature conservative, or don't want to make a mistake, add a little pizzazz to a basic fabric plan by using a different or unusual fabric on pillows or accessories or a small item. If you tire of it or find you can't live with your choice, you can always make a change without drastically affecting your pocketbook or the rest of your room.

Also, note that some large samples of fabrics in stores and upholstery showrooms display co-ordinates right on the sample in smaller swatches. This can be a great help in choosing companions to your main selection. If you are in doubt or nervous about "going it alone", this is an easy and safe way to decorate. The sample size you see is also important. A small piece of the fabric may look very different from the larger piece you will require on your furniture. Ask for a larger sample or a picture of the fabric actually made up on something, if available.

41. What window treatments are "in" and what kinds go with what style?

On the following pages are some window treatments popularly used today. Some are clearly traditional, others contemporary. Many fall in both categories according to fabric choices.

Window treatments are functional (providing privacy) as well as decorative. Often times, more than one window treatment must be used to fill the need.

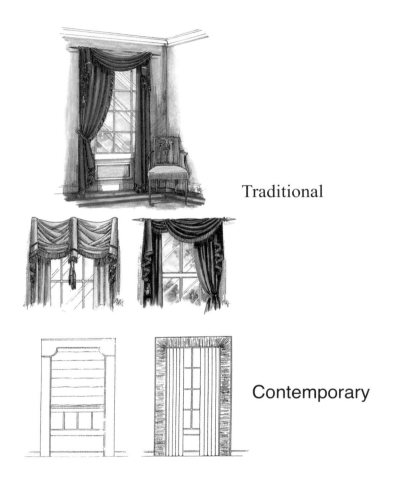

Traditional

Contemporary

Reprinted with permission from:
The Encyclopedia of Window Fashions
Charles T. Randall
Illustrations by
Patricia M. Howard

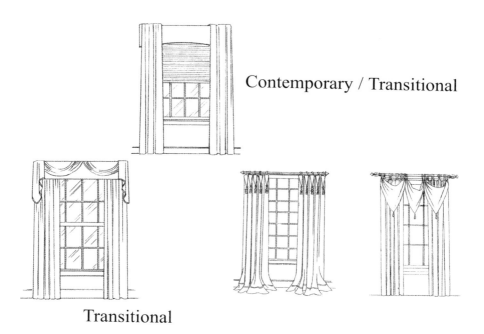

Contemporary / Transitional

Transitional

Traditional / Transitional

Eclectic

(39)

Chapter V

Walls and Wall Coverings

42. How do walls function in my design plan?

We take them for granted, but walls affect our furnishings and design scheme when they are there and when they are not! Generally, walls act as a backdrop for patterns on furniture or flooring, but not always. There are times when the walls become the focal point and the rest of the room becomes more subdued.

43. What about defects such as obstructions, jogs, and boxed-out areas?

Many apartment dwellers, as well as homeowners, have had to "work around" such wall spoilers. Generally, architectural defects should be treated exactly as the wall-whether the wall is painted, papered or paneled. Sometimes, however, they can be turned into an interesting design feature by a little creativity and imagination. For example, beams become fluted columns, jogs, when built out, become niches, a boxed-out area near the ceiling can become an attractive border element. Most times, however, you want them to go away, so let them blend in and forget them.

44. What type of wall applications do I have to choose from?

There are many options such as paint and decorative paint techniques, wallpaper (from full walls to borders), wood application and wood paneling, fabrics, mirrors, stone (marble, granite), brick, ceramic tile and even metal. Each serves a purpose and has a different effect on a room design.

45. What architectural features are used on walls?

The basic architectural features are moldings, fireplaces, windows and doors. Doing nothing else to the walls but painting them may be enough, if these architectural elements are important. The use of ceiling moldings (crown), chair rail (dado cap) and base moldings add character to a room as well as interest. Ceiling and floor moldings can be used in traditional and country setting as well as contemporary, while chair rails are used mainly for the former.

Fireplaces can be the focal point of a wall, or an entire room. It's finish (brick, stone, granite, marble) can set the tone, style and color scheme. It can be accented by a beautiful wood mantel and help create a period room setting from American Federal to Neo Classic Louis XVI. It can also function as an architectural element without being a major focal point, as in a contemporary or Southwestern design, by using stucco, marble or simple sheetrock to blend in with the rest of the wall.

Doors and windows today have come into their own from various and sundry sizes to unique shapes. This has occurred because of the revival of many Neoclassic, Victorian and post-modern styles of architecture, as well as continued interest in contemporary dwellings featuring large glass elements and lots of light. Windows - round, rectangular and even triangular, dressed or undressed can be a major focal point in a room. They not only emphasize and define space, but bring the outside in. Doors, available to match any style and décor, likewise, bring instant elegance to a bland, featureless structure.

But what if a home lacks interesting or important moldings or doors, or you don't want them featured? Instead of creating a focal point by staining or painting them a different color than the walls, paint them the same so that they blend in rather than stand out.

46. What options do I have in choosing wallpaper?

The choices are so many and varied today that you really must consider your room design and style, color schemes, fabrics and flooring when shopping. Do you want the walls patterned or textured? Do you want borders or chair rails?

Wall coverings are used to create many effects, and they

can be practical as well, especially the vinyls today which are not only washable, but scrubbable. So consider how you want your room to look when it is complete. Do you want the walls to act as a backdrop for artwork, or do you want your walls to co-ordinate or repeat the fabric patterns? Do you want the room to appear larger and more spacious, or cozier and more intimate?

From contemporary woven looks to period moiré (a pattern that looks like water marks), textural wall coverings create interest without using busy patterns in a room. They can, in lighter colors, enlarge a room visually, and in darker tones, create drama and effect. Textural wall coverings can be used in conjunction with patterns as well (i.e., a traditional dining room can feature a silk-look wall covering above a chair rail, and a floral or stripe companion wall covering below the chair rail).

Many wall coverings have accompanying fabrics. Some even offer upholstery-weight textiles, as well as coordinating cottons. Be aware, however, that the color match is never guaranteed. Check the samples carefully. If they aren't close enough in color, know that the actual product will have the same variations. Options include selecting a companion stripe (less colors than floral), or consider using the fabric further away from the paper (such as on dining room chairs, rather than on the window treatment).

In contemporary rooms today, when wallpaper is considered, textures of all kinds have superceded the once very popular foils and mylars. Contemporary-looking screen prints are still popular for baths, kitchens and bedrooms. Painted wall effects (such as sponge or string painting) are more popular in entry, living room, dining room and great room spaces because of varying ceiling heights and open spaces where it is difficult to know where to end the wallpaper. Traditional rooms are being enhanced by wall coverings that stimulate and are inspired by patterns of the past in original and contrasting colors. Stripes, florals, combinations of both, and companion borders are very popular and bring warmth and charm to kitchens, dining rooms, foyers, bedrooms, baths and almost any room in the house. A laser cutting process has even allowed borders to have unusual shapes and scallops. They are easy to install despite their designs, and give a unique effect at little cost.

Novelty papers, trends, sports, 50's nostalgia, etc. are just that - a novelty. They can be fun and cute, but generally people rapidly tire of them. This doesn't mean they shouldn't be used. As long as they are strippable for easy removal, the walls are well prepared, and their cost and installation is not exorbitant, go for it, knowing that this is not a long-lasting look.

Painting or papering one wall or more differently may create a special effect, but if it looks contrived or disturbs the unity of the floor plan, forget it.

47. How do I know how much wallpaper to buy?

Wallpaper is generally sold in two- or three-roll bolts. Each roll of wallpaper is generally 27" wide and some European papers measure 21" wide. Contract or commercial wall coverings, generally available through a designer, are often sold in yards rather than rolls, and measure 36" or 54" wide (like fabric).

If you are planning to hire a wallpaper hanger, ask the installer to give you the number of rolls or yardage he or she will need to do the job properly. It is often practical to order a little extra in case of future damages (later dye lots will never be the same, and the screens may become unavailable). If you are planning to install it yourself, check pattern repeat and matching instructions, as well as width. As a general rule of thumb, measure the length of the walls, multiply by the height of the ceiling and divide by 30. This will give you a little more than you need because you have not taken out for windows and doors. A large repeat will also increase the amount of rolls you need to purchase.

In determining the amount of border paper, add up the lineal (running) feet of the walls to be covered. Most borders are sold in 5 yard bolts (or 15'). You must always order full bolts, so chances are, you will be over a few feet. The cost of borders is usually not great, and you might find an additional use for the few extra feet (wall appliqués for added effect). If you are using the border at the ceiling, as well as for a chair rail, don't forget to double the amount.

In hanging wallpaper, have wall conditions checked because the prep work is as important as the paper hanging for the end result. The walls may also require a liner paper, which, when hung horizontally, avoids it's seams meeting the wallpaper seams.

48. What options do I have with paint?

Paint colors number in the thousands as paint companies' color charts will attest. Background colors from fabrics or carpets are generally the way wall colors are selected.

Paint finishes such as flat (dull finishes), used in main areas, glossy (shiny finishes) used for woodwork, doors and frames and rooms like bathrooms and kitchens, and semi-gloss (not as shiny as gloss but more durable than flat) used for woodworking when high shine is not appropriate, are common choices and create different effects, as well as serve different purposes.

Gloss and eggshell finishes on walls are also choices, but show imperfections and should be used judiciously.

Sponge, marbleized and striated painting are techniques which are popular in both contemporary and traditional homes, depending on which you choose. The topcoat applied makes the walls practical and cleanable. Custom colors, alone or in combination with one another, allow great diversity. When selecting one of these painting techniques, always view a large enough sample or the finished walls may not be what you expected.

Wonderful painted effects are popular today through stenciling (an old craft that is getting renewed interest) and mural art, often called trompe l'oeil (literally translated to mean "trick of the eye"). Artists can create springtime all year round, put you inside an aquarium, and create windows and what's going on outside them - all on blank walls. From formal settings (i.e. dining rooms and hallways) to whimsical environments (in kid's rooms or baths), these painted effects can even make you believe there is wood molding and furniture where there really isn't.

If you have some artistic ability, you might consider trying these projects on your own. If not, there are many talented professionals today who can do the job.

49. What effect does fabric have on walls?

Fabric can be applied to walls by paper backing it and hanging it like wallpaper, or by different upholstery methods. One method is to use firring strips to mount the fabric onto the wall. Another is to staple the fabric directly and frame it with wood moldings to cover the staples. A third is to use batting such as upholstery fill under the fabric, which is sewn, stretched and stapled. The job is completed by gluing fabric welting over the staples to create a finished, upholstered look.

Fabric on walls creates a rich, soft, elegant effect. It can also act as a sound reducer as well as a warmth retainer. If you are handy, many wall effects with fabric are easier than painting. In addition, you can change the wall effects when you change windows or slipcovers and have a whole new look. Bedroom sheets can be used as fabric on walls to give a coordinated look, as well.

50. What effect does wood have on walls?

The look of wood applications whether traditional or contemporary, always lends character to a room. Nothing makes a traditional library more special than oak or mahogany walls to compliment bookcases and built-ins. In combination with fine wall coverings or wall fabrics, a dado of wood (wood applied below the chair rail) along with ceiling and floor moldings creates a classic room which never goes out of style. The use of pine and maple create a warm and cozy country effect. Walls of oak and ash, anigre, mahogany, rosewood or other exotic woods can enhance a contemporary décor by adding texture and warmth. Moldings may also be incorporated, but the profiles should not look colonial or traditional. Accents of lacquers or metals can be used.

51. What other products are used on walls?

In rooms such as baths and kitchens, tile can create a practical and beautiful effect. Ceramic tile, porcelain and tumbled marble with accents, inserts or feature strips, give a designer look to part or all of bathroom walls, and sitting rooms, as well as backsplashes in kitchens.

Mirrors, both clear and tinted, enlarge spaces and create a wonderful backdrop for many furniture styles, as well as camouflaging negative features of walls. Similarly, stone or brick, as well as metal (copper, stainless steel, hammered brass) are materials that can be used for special effects. You must remember, however, that walls must be appropriately prepared or supported (and sometimes floors) for each product and this should be done by professionals.

Area rugs create "islands" for seating or demark entry foyers in an open space plan. Note the complimentary step carpet.

Built in cabinetry can provide multifunctional space for bar, storage, T.V. components and still allow for sofa seating in a room with little wall space.

An eclectic feeling permeates this essentially contemporary room because of the area rug and window treatments.

Color and tone are set by this highly stylized rug offsetting the neutrals and art work.

A small kitchen is brightened by painted and glazed cabinetry with lots of storage. Antique fixtures create warmth and ambiance.

This large kitchen has a bi-level island to accommodate additional chairs for the refectory kitchen table which opens to seat at least 10.

Painted and glazed wood built-ins with pop up T.V. create a spacious and uncluttered feeling in this average size master bedroom.

Vibrant color creates impact in a guest bedroom with a flair. Crown moldings and trim in crisp white accentuate this color pallete.

An unforgettable garden is created in this powder room by the artistic use of trompe l'oeil (literal translation - "trick of the eye").

Paneled walls, computer desk and bookcase turn this library/T.V./ guest room (sleep sofa) into a well designed multi-functional space.

Paneled walls, wood floors, antique oriental rugs and period furniture create a timeless Manhattan apartment.

A state of the art flat screen T.V. was placed over existing brick fireplace covered with new cabinetry for display and storage, creating a fresh look with more function.

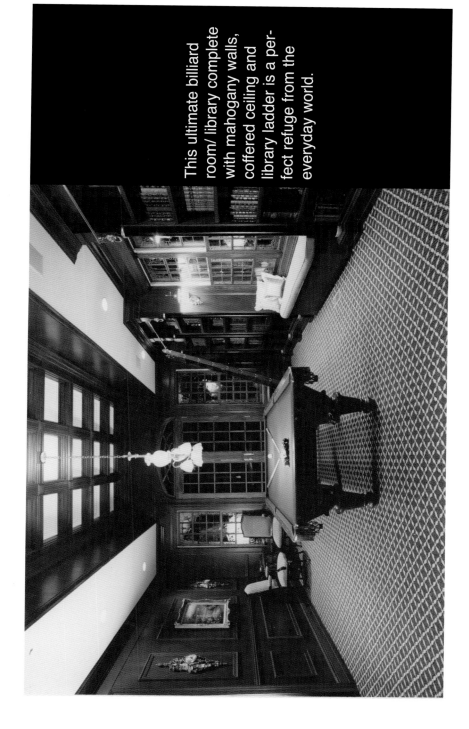

This ultimate billiard room/ library complete with mahogany walls, coffered ceiling and library ladder is a perfect refuge from the everyday world.

Porcelain flooring throughout the main living area, with entry foyer medallion focal point, gives a sense of flow and largesse to this average size condo.

An open space plan is conducive to comfortable conversation and T.V. watching. Custom built-ins provide plenty of storage, as well as bar area, surrounding the fireplace.

A romantic sitting room, as part of a master bedroom, includes built-ins and electric fireplace. It's a perfect get-a-way for reading and T.V. watching, as well as being together.

Chapter VI

Floor Coverings

52. What kinds of floor coverings are available to choose from and how do you determine what to use where?

Flooring, usually divided into carpeting and hard surface materials, runs the gamut from wall-to-wall carpeting, area rugs, wood, ceramic, stone, slate, brick, marble, granite and terrazzo, with vinyl and other composition tile and linoleum somewhere in between.

To determine which to use, ask the following questions:

Will this product be practical in the space, as well as be the right look ?

How will the floor selections look when they meet one another?

What will the maintenance entail?

Am I making the best choice, design-wise and price-wise?

53. What should I know about choices for wall-to-wall carpet?

Wall-to-wall carpet, or broadloom, is available in many different textures in wool, nylon and other synthetics (acrylic, polyester, olefin) as well as combinations of these (fabric content must be listed on the label). The pile or texture of the carpet creates certain effects. Cut pile can be high (shag), or low (commercial), or in between (plush-like velvet). Uncut pile (looped), like Berber, is another choice, as well as a combination of cut and uncut (random sheared). Sculptured and carved carpets are examples of patterned carpets produced by pile height differences.

Each type of carpet, in the appropriate color and pattern, can enhance a room greatly. As a budget item whose price is directly proportionate to quality and longevity, it is important to get the best your budget can afford.

The key to carpet selection is to fit the type to the space. For example, a lovely dense plush carpet might do wonders for the look of a living or dining room, but would not wear well on steps because of smiling (when the carpet shows a crease where it folds) or matting down. Conversely, a tight-looped carpet or flat sculpture would be ideal for steps, but may not be "rich" enough for formal spaces.

Mixing pile heights in different rooms that are visible to one another is often done today, as well as using different pile heights as accents or inserts in the same room. The key to unity is style and color coordination.

54. How do you measure for carpeting?

Carpeting is generally sold installed and priced by the yard. You can estimate it's cost by measuring the length and the width of a room (including closets) to get square feet and then divide by 9 to get square yards.

For example, a family room measures 18' x 25': (18 x 25 = 450 divided by 9 = 50 sq. yds.) If the carpet costs $30 per yard installed, the cost estimate is $1500 (50 yards @ $30/yd). But there are other things to consider as well. Does the price include padding, and since there are different grades, is it the grade you want? Are there additional labor charges (steps, rip-up, floor preparation)? Do you want to order extra for step replacement, area rugs, etc? Is the carpet you selected sold by the square yard? Some custom carpets are sold and priced by the lineal foot. Most carpets are sold in 12' or 15' widths. Make sure you aren't getting a carpet where you are paying for a lot of waste (unless you plan to use it elsewhere).

Ask the carpet dealer to show you a layout of the room

Ask the carpet dealer to show you a layout of the room so that you can see where he has put the seams. A good plan will not waste carpet, but will not have seams prominent in main areas or walkways.

55. What should I know about oriental rugs, types, coordination, size and color?

Oriental rugs enhance everyone's home whether contemporary or traditional, old or new. When cared for, they can be used, enjoyed and passed on from generation to generation as family heirlooms no matter what the price.

Different styles of rugs can be used in varying room settings, as well as in the same room. Persian styles such as Kashan, Tabriz and Heriz which are boldly patterned, are ideal for dens, entries and other trafficked areas because of their overall patterns, but can certainly be featured in living room or dining rooms for formal or informal settings. Chinese rugs can be used in most areas as well, depending on pattern and coverage, and generally create a more formal setting. Particularly elegant in living room, dining room and master bedroom suites or in a large foyer area, these types of rugs can act as a catalyst for most traditional styles of furniture. Dhurries and Kilims are generally more informal, working well with contemporary designs. Do not be confused between the country of origin and the style. Often times a classic style (Persian Kashan, for example) will be produced on looms in China or India. Always ask because it affects the value, especially if you are interested in antique rugs.

Needlepoints have become popular, with the resurgence of period-style furniture, particularly English and French. Many reproduction needlepoints echo the beauty of the past, often with more clarity than the originals. Nourmak, an antique replica, is another type of rug enjoying great popularity. Everyone seems to want something new that looks old. Another trend is acid washing a new rug to give it an "old" look.

Area rugs with varying patterns can be effectively mixed. The key is coordination of color and scale. A good rule of thumb is to decide what the basic color or colors are in one carpet and look for them as background colors in your second or third rug. Go for the "blend", not the "match". For example, a large-scale floral can mix well with geometrics or simple border designs, provided the colors work together. In fact, design novices can put together a fairly sophisticated room using solid colors elsewhere and basic furniture, allowing the "fabulous floors" to create the effect.

The size of a rug creates the parameters of a space, whether it be the room at large, or a conversational seating area. The former acts as broadloom, in effect, since it's almost wall-to-wall coverage puts all furniture on it. The latter creates subtle subdivisions of space that can enhance the room's diversity and create interest or drama, particularly where the furniture arrangement is basic, or the setting bland. For example, a small area rug under a cocktail table can create a cozy and inviting feeling in a conversation area with sofas and pull up chairs. The same seating arrangement will come into focus as a major area of importance with a large area rug under all of it.

As you already know, color is the one decorative element that psychologically and subliminally creates effect. Bright bold colors promote drama and focus in a space, making it appear to come toward you. Soft, subtle colors create a calmer, more restful feeling, blending the environment, allowing the area to recede. The same is often true of rug patterns: Persian, Indian or Kilim rugs fill the space. If they are in bold or dark in color, they demand further attention. Yet it is interesting to note that the most heavily patterned carpet can appear soft and subtle in restful monochromatic colors. Conversely, a carved Chinese rug with a simple border and small medallion can take center stage in vibrant colors.

By far, the most important step in purchasing a rug is selecting a store whose quality and integrity are well established. Choosing a professional firm with a top reputation helps guarantee that it is a genuine handmade oriental rug. When shopping, be ready to describe the desired size and color range, and by all means, tell the dealer in what room the rug will be placed. Because an oriental rug is an investment meant to last a lifetime, it is best to furnish the room around it. However, if that's too impractical, take along fabric samples of existing furniture and draperies, and even a photo of the space where it will be used.

56. What about creating designer looks through other area rugs and wall-to-wall carpets?

Years ago, area rugs were of the Oriental or traditional kind, woven or tufted, made by hand or machine. In the last few decades, the broadloom industry has gotten on the bandwagon and provided area rugs for more contemporary settings by cutting various carpet materials into patterns and heat setting them together with a backing. This process has made wall-to-wall carpeting much more versatile as well. Now border inserts can be put into step carpet, patterned areas can be inserted into living room/dining room broadloom, and any room that has wall-to-wall carpeting can have a designer accent inserted into it.

This process can be used to create a new look in your existing carpeting, if the carpet is not worn and is dense enough. The carpet is removed from the tackless, the new area inserted, using part of the old or all new, and is heat set in from the reverse side. Then the carpet is reinstalled.

Another interesting designer effect is carving. Often, carving is incorporated into insert work because it defines and delineates the color and patterns. It is accomplished by using a beveling machine (a large version of the tool that shaves sideburns). Carving also eliminates the rug yarns from one color from falling over onto another and creating lines that look uneven. Carving or sculpting can only be accomplished when the yarn is dense. It can create a beautiful look even when used in solid wall-to-wall carpet. Picture how effective a carved floral pattern, can be under a glass coffee table or at the corners of a dining table.

Computers have also taken over the carpet industry, and rug programs give choices of many different styles of area rugs in various colors you select. Because these can be mass-produced, they become the most cost effective. The cost will increase if you choose custom colors and designs.

57. When should you consider wood floors?

Whether for contemporary or traditional homes, people today appreciate the beauty of wood flooring. In the last decades, wood floors were often covered by broadloom. Today, many new home builders offer carpet over subflooring and charge additionally for wood.

There are many interesting effects that can be created with wood. Standard patterns, such as planks (random or uniform), parquet (basketweave) or checkerboard (grains running opposite one another), have been modified and customized by sanding, bleaching, staining, sealing and inserting inlays, as well as installing them on the diagonal. This versatility enables much creative use of a natural product, which is practical as well as beautiful. Wood can be more easily maintained today with improved floor preparations and can always be sanded and redone for the long haul.

Wood cannot be used where there is moisture, therefore, never use it below ground level. It may not be practical for everyone in kitchens, although wood look-alikes in vinyl and tile have solved that problem. There are also prefinished wood veneer floors available in several colors, but they cannot be resanded often because the wood is only a thin layer on the surface and doesn't have the depth of solid wood.

Today, wood is most popular in conjunction with the use of area rugs and is sometimes preferred over hard surface floors such as ceramic, marble or granite because it is not as slippery or hard to stand on (especially in homes with young children). By protecting it with polyurethane or similar products (which don't necessarily have to be shiny), wood becomes a practical and versatile surface. Stenciling and other floor-painted decorations can give a unique designer look from country to contemporary styles.

58. When and where are ceramic, porcelain and other hard surface floors a consideration?

Hard surface flooring is most commonly used in hallways, kitchens, bathrooms, around fireplaces and other areas where moisture, dirt and extensive wear and tear occur. The decorative effects are virtually limitless in terms of patterns, shapes and colors. The installation of these products in mud or thinset is not as simple as changing your carpet, so select with care and for longevity For this reason, stay away from busy patterns that you may grow tired of, and stick to colors that are basic. (You might also want to think about resale). In addition, area rugs and wall coverings, as well as patterned fabrics, should be able to coordinate well with your choice, even if you want to change your color scheme later on.

59. Are vinyls a good choice today?

Vinyls have returned in popularity today and run the gamut from sheet material to varying tile shapes. These floors are glued down with adhesive and are not as thick as ceramics and marble. For this reason, they make an excellent product for use in kitchens where there is existing cabinetry and appliances. A thicker product would "land lock" the appliances and make them impossible to remove for service or replacement.

There are a variety of vinyl choices in wood and hard surface simulants as well as countless colors and textures. Floor dressings and cleaners allow maintenance to be easy. If you're looking for the "real thing", vinyl may not be for you - but examine the possibilities. This product has come a long way since the 70's.

60. What about granite and marble?

Their popularity is great today for flooring, countertops and in bathrooms, but beware. Marble is ill advised for many heavy-trafficked halls and not practical for countertops. While marble floors can be wet sanded to repair (a messy and expensive project), it scratches and stains and can be a very slippery surface. It's beauty, however, like granite, cannot be denied. Granite is generally preferred, because it is a stronger product, less apt to stain and scratch.

Tumbled marble, limestone and porcelain products (both polished and unpolished) are creating "new-old" looks which are most practical and attractive, some in popular price ranges.

Before making your selections, consider that your choice will be one that you will live with for a long time. Make sure it is what you want tomorrow, as well as today, and that it fits the needs of your chosen space.

Chapter VII

Lighting

61. Why is lighting so important?

Lighting is a key factor in any room. Its effects can literally "light up your life" or create "doom and gloom". It can flatter people, furnishings and artwork or have the opposite effect. Artificial lighting must be considered along with natural light (windows, skylites, etc.), and color selections for your rooms should be made after checking how they look both by day and night lighting. Lighting can and should be an interesting blend of many types of light sources - fixtures, high hats, lamps, sconces - all of which can be used in both traditional and contemporary settings.

62. What kinds of lighting choices are there?

There are a variety of choices. Used properly, they help people see well, as well as enhance furnishings. General lighting (diffused light) can be recessed (high hats or eye balls) as well as incandescent and fluorescent ceiling-mounted or suspended fixtures (many today have halogen light bulbs). Also available are track lights, cove lighting, ceiling fixtures, and lamps for floors, tables and desks. These direct and indirect lighting sources fulfill function as well as create a mood.

63. When is recessed lighting used?

Recessed lighting, the most popular kind used in many homes, both with traditional and contemporary architecture, creates overall lighting that is unobtrusive and can be placed to strategically light seating areas and task areas. It is not necessarily ideal reading light. Most need at least 6-8" of depth to install and are even made today for cathedral ceilings. Eyeballs, which have the capacity to swivel, can create more direct light on walls as well. Both high hats and eyeballs usually come in white, black, chrome and brass, and are most desirable when the lighting blends into the ceiling. They can also be used in conjunction with other ceiling mounted light sources, such as chandeliers.

64. Are ceiling fixtures "in"?

Chandeliers have become very popular, once again, with the reawakening of interest in traditional French and English furniture styles. Beautiful antiques and reproduction pieces are available in varying price ranges. There are many contemporary glass, brass and iron fixtures as well as eclectic and neo-classic styles (a new twist to the old classical style). Ceiling fixtures can be used with high hats or eyeballs and are most effective over dining room, kitchen or game tables and in foyer areas and bathrooms, provided they stay with the feeling and style of the furniture or other light sources.

65. How do lamps and sconces enhance the lighting in a room?

Visual beauty in a room can be created by lamps and sconces, as well as filling the practical need of good reading light. They are available in many styles and finishes, both new and antique. Sconces (wall-mounted fixtures) can also be practical light sources. For example, there may not be enough room for a table lamp or standing light (torchière) beside a wing chair next to a fireplace. A wall sconce can create the perfect reading light and at the same time, fill a decorative need. The same is true for bedroom lighting. Sometimes night tables are too small or used for items other than lamps. Sconces or swing arm wall mounted fixtures are the perfect problem solver.

Table lamps create warmth in a room which is not only due to its light giving potential. They soften their surroundings and create a glow that can enrich fabrics and wall coverings in a way that ceiling-mounted lighting cannot. They also illuminate desk areas and reading spaces more effectively.

66. What other lighting effects are there?

Track lighting is a great asset in areas where the depth to install high hats or eyeballs is unavailable. It gives the added advantage of relocating the fixtures along the track at any time to highlight a new art piece, rearrange the furniture, or simply increase or reduce the amount of light.

Fluorescent lighting, while not the most popular choice of homeowners today, is still used in areas where bright light is necessary (kitchen, laundry, garage, basement, attic, etc.). Some people find that it's slight hum is a detriment, but it doesn't bother everyone and flourescents have improved considerably, today. Fluorescent tubes under kitchen cabinets provide good counter light and create a nice effect. Dimmers are available today for many fluorescents.

Cove lighting creates a soft glow and is considered "mood lighting". It can be accomplished by varying types of tubing (neon, fluorescent or incandescent) at the ceiling, covered by a molding, bracket or soffit. The light source is not visible, just the glow is. Color effects may also be accomplished by using different bulb colors.

Lighting can even be created under water, or in carpeting, through the use of fiber optics (tiny strands that when woven together create varying patterns of light, with the use of a transformer). This is a relatively new and interesting field that affords many options and effects.

There are also special fixtures that are specifically used for framing artwork or focusing on a specific area. These cannot be purchased at every lighting store, and must be installed by a knowledgeable electrician at the correct distance to function properly.

67. What about watts and bulbs?

Wattage in incandescent bulbs (bulbs that have a filament) ranges from 15 (diameter) to 300 watts (very bright). As the wattage increases, so does the light, and bulbs of 150 watts, for example, are brighter than two 75 watt bulbs. Three-way bulbs have two filaments and can produce lighting such as 50-100-150 watts (as in lamps). Fluorescent light containing mercury in a phosphorescent tube provides much more wattage than incandescent. Its wattage is related to the length of the tube and therefore fixed. Both incandescent and many fluorescent fixtures can work on dimmer switches, which allow for different levels of light for effect and use. Most people upgrade their existing electrical plan with this product, as well as consider it in new design work.

Bulb shapes differ as well as socket sizes, so always check the lamp or fixture. If a fixture specifies wattage, do not go over that wattage for safety reasons. If it will not give enough light for your needs, select another.

Bulb colors differ from frosted and clear to blue white, yellow white and bright white. Tinted bulbs are also available. Each will have its own effect on fabrics, furniture, wall coverings and wood.

68. What about halogen?

Halogen lighting is a newer invention in bulbs. The bulb is very small and can be easily damaged by the oils from your hands. The advantage of halogen in contemporary lighting is that the fixture can be sleek and decorative, since the bulb takes up little space. Since it can get very hot, it should not be placed where clothing or anything flammable can touch the bulb.

69. Is neon an option in residences?

Neon tubing, as a continuous light source which can be bent to shape and is available in different colors, is most often used commercially for signs and lighting effects in restaurants, catering halls and stores. It is breakable and not often used below chair level. The use of neon in residential design is primarily to create lighting effects in bars, planters and for cove lighting, since in most cases the glow is what is desired, not the visibility of the tube.

70. What is a lighting plan?

A lighting plan, essential to any room design, is generally done by overlaying a transparent piece of paper on the furniture floor plan and marking the location of the different sources of light. Marking the desired light sources on a second furniture plan is another way. Fixtures, high hats, eyeballs, track lights, lamps and sconces are marked differently, as are switch and outlet locations.

For the lay person, however, a simpler plan is sufficient, but necessary. Since lighting should be diverse and interesting, but also functional, the plan should reflect the location of all the above-mentioned light sources you choose to use in the room. Don't become overzealous and make your ceiling look like swiss cheese, but be aware that it is important to locate general and specific lighting where needed in your furniture layout.

Chapter VIII

Woods and Wood Furniture

71. What is the difference between wood furniture and micas?

Wood furniture, obviously, is made by using a real wood product. Often times, it is a combination of solid wood parts and veneers (a thin layer of the same wood applied over ply-wood, particle board or another solid wood) to avoid warping. Micas or laminates are man-made products usually 1/16 or 1/32 of an inch thick, which are applied to particleboard or plywood. They come in hundreds of varieties, colors, textures and even wood simulants, and are produced by many different companies which have similar products. Both wood and mica veneers can be purchased already applied to 4' x 8' sheets of material, (or custom order sizes) for use on flat surfaces.

72. Is a veneer not as good as solid wood?

In some cases, using a veneer avoids warping or racking, particularly on cabinet doors, and is an accepted practice. It is not necessarily used to cheapen the finished product. Actually using veneering in the period styles of the past was an art. Inlays were used (small pieces of different types of woods fash-ioned to create a pattern or design set flush with the surface). Marquetry is another term for this procedure, which was very popular in England, France and America in the late 1700 and early 1800's, as well as other western European countries.

With wood flooring, however, the fact that a veneer is used over another product means that the wear surface is still only 1/16 of an inch thick (as in many prefinished wood floors). Practically speaking, if your floor will need to be sanded and refinished many times because of great use, a solid wood floor would be the appropriate choice.

73. What kinds of woods are popular today with the general public?

With the return of traditional styles as a popular design theme, after a recent past of contemporary furniture made of micas, or woods such as beech, birch or oak, woods such as maple, cherry, poplar, walnut and mahogany are becoming more visible. These hardwoods can be finished in color ranges from whites and creams to deep reds and wines, and their grains make them distinctive.

Contemporary furniture today sometimes uses woods on particleboard and applies a highly-polished finish such as polyurethane to create a sleek, glossy look. Marbleizing and other faux finishes are often created as an option to seeing the grain of the wood.

74. How does the type of wood affect the style of the furniture?

Traditional furniture, French, English, and American, employed certain woods for   different styles. For example, early 17th century styles used a great deal of oak. Later, refined styles in the 18th century used mahogany and satinwood. Early styles in America used local woods such as oak, maple, and cherry. Later styles used walnut and mahogany. If authentic reproductions are what you are looking for, it is important to use the woods that were used then. If you're seeking the look, but not the exact interpretation, you have more latitude. Grain and color adaptability are the major factors in determining choice.

Whether on walls (wainscoting) or furniture, fine woods, beautifully made and well installed, provide elegance and time-less style to any décor.

75. How does the color of the wood affect the décor?

Lighter woods, like lighter colored walls tend to open up a space and make it appear larger. Similarly, darker woods on furniture or wall applications tend to enclose a space, making it smaller or more intimate.

Darker woods and painted finishes predominate certain styles. We have the choice of lightening these same woods by bleaching or pickling (oak and ash are good candidates).

A combination of light and dark woods are also most effective and certain types of Art Deco and Modern furniture combine these in inlays and mosaic patterns.

Whatever the choice of color, be sure it enhances the wood itself. Mahogany is a classic example of a fine wood that looks beautiful in all its tones of reds and wines, as well as natural. To lighten and bleach it, would lose its inherent beauty. Other woods such as ash, oak, and bird's eye maple look better in lighter tones so that the unique and interesting grain is highlighted.

76.When would you use a custom cabinet shop?

The very word "custom" gives you the answer. Custom furniture is an option when ready-made isn't the solution for your design problem and you wish to maximize every inch of space. It is a solution, as well, if you choose to create something which is not mass produced but individualized for your needs, taste, and pocketbook. Many designers work with custom cabinet shops for this reason, but some shops have a design staff to help you if you go it alone. A custom woodworking shop can also provide and install full wood wall paneling as well as moldings, columns, niches, etc.

77. When dealing with a woodworking shop, how do you know you'll get what you ordered?

You must request concept sketches for pricing and then after field measuring your project, ask for shop drawings which show elevations and floor plans. Be sure you understand what you are looking at before you sign your approval and give your deposit. Make sure the wood is listed, as well as handles, trim, etc. It would also be a good idea to have the delivery time in writing. This will ensure that a 10-12 week delivery promise doesn't turn into six months.

78. How important is the cabinet construction to you?

Cabinetry construction is as important as good looks. Some people don't agree until they open a drawer that falls off it's glide or try to close doors that don't line up exactly. Remember, most people don't change their furniture every few years. Chances are, you will have yours for more than 10-15 years after purchase, whether you think so or not when you buy it.

So buy the best quality you can afford. Check out the products and don't be misled by glitzy style which can cover shoddy workmanship. Also remember, if it doesn't look good on the showroom floor, your new delivery won't be any better when it arrives. Save money by buying less, but wisely, and in the long run it will stand the test of time and good quality.

79. What about refinishing existing wood furniture?

Professionally refinishing old or worn wood furniture is not inexpensive, but may be worthwhile. Good quality furniture, prized because it is a family heirloom or just because it has special meaning, can look like new or better when refinished properly. There are many "do it yourself" kits on the market, as well, if your budget won't allow for professional help, but be aware that the end result will not be the same. While the task is labor intensive in part, the large spray booths and industrial products used by professional refinishing companies do make a difference. If an old piece of furniture is well made, even though it is not an antique, give it its due, and it will give you many more years of good service and beauty.

80. How do you maintain fine wood furniture?

Using a clean cloth and a small amount of water can keep your furniture looking lovely without oily or shiny wax buildup. Since wood breathes and absorbs moisture from the air, the biggest danger is that it will get dried out. By adding moisture back in small amounts, the natural beauty and luster of a fine wood piece will be maintained.

Chapter IX

Art and Art Accessories

81. What do accessories do for a room?

EVERYONE!

Whether a large budget or small, fine furniture or not, accessories give a room personality and are the finishing touches that turn a furniture collection into a lovely and gracious home. Often, people don't consider the cost for these finishing touches in their overall budget plan or think they are of minor importance, but nothing can be further from the truth. So accessories must be chosen with great care, for they will surely make the difference in your design project.

82. Why is it difficult for most people to accessorize?

There are many elements of good design that go into choosing the appropriate accessory - style, color, size, proximity to other accessories and a sense of balance. It takes time and sometimes trial and error. What looks good in the store may not necessarily have the same effect in your home. Many times professionals need to be called in to complete a room successfully.

83. What are functional accessories?

Functional accessories are objects that not only look good while complimenting chairs, tables and other furniture, but are also filling a need. Such functional accessories are lighting fixtures, fireplace equipment, clocks, mirrors, decorative hardware, vases, books and pillows. When well selected, they lend a personal touch and appear to blend well with their environment. When ill-chosen, they will either fail to create the needed compliment to a completed whole, or worse, attract your eye as a negative force.

84. What are decorative accessories?

Decorative accessories are provided more for appearance than functional need. But they often fill other, more psychological needs. Art, such as paintings and sculpture, fall into this category. The nesting instinct, as well as the "desire to acquire", is fulfilled, making your home a reflection of your own personal good taste, as well as a place to live and hang your hat.

85. What are collectibles?

The very word defines the acquisitional need in many of us. Whether collecting bottle caps, baseball cards or dolls when we were kids, or the very same when we got older, for different reasons (perhaps to recapture our past childhood), people love to collect things from their travels, as well as their personal interests or hobbies. Such items may be of monetary value or not, but they are important to the collector. They also make wonderful accessories to personalize a space. Showcasing them is the challenging part and should be made to compliment the rest of the décor while not overshadowing it.

86. What is considered "art"?

The world of art is a vast and beautiful one to explore. Whether your interest is paintings (traditional, contemporary in oils, watercolors or other media) or sculpture (bronzes, woods, three-dimensional objects made from garden tools), art has been with us through the ages from prehistoric cave paintings (telling the story of daily life through pictures) to the abstract world of collages and non-representative shapes and forms. Posters, lithographs and serigraphs are also considered art.

Art, whether the collection is worthy of being displayed in a museum or not, is generally selected more for personal taste than investment. Although people enjoy the quest as well as the result, such accessories lend a special touch to a home.

Art does not have to "match" the décor. In truth, such accessories seem to lose their artistic value rather than enhance the space when they "match". They should be appropriately placed, sized well for the selected wall, and hung at the right height for viewing. If the color values blend, that is an added plus. Form can coordinate with the furniture style, but need not. For example, a fine collection of contemporary art is not out of place in a traditional home.

87. How do you know how high to hang artwork?

The rule of thumb has been to hang artwork so that it is at eye level when standing, but many designers and professionals prefer to place art slightly above eye level when seated. Generally, this is no more than 8" -10" above sofas or low units such as consoles, credenzas or tables. This not only enables the art to be viewed more effectively, but creates a cohesive arrangement with the furnishings surrounding it.

Groupings have become popular again. If you are unsure of how to place the pieces, use the floor! Lay out all the objects on the floor in the same amount of space as on the wall. Move the pieces until they create a pleasing and unified presentation. Measure their locations and then hang them. If you want to be very sure, take a large piece of paper and trace the location of the pieces, marking where the wires will fall to the bottom of your picture hook. (Using two hooks together enables the art to hang better). Then put the paper on the wall with easy to remove masking tape. Put up all hooks in marked locations. Remove the paper and hang the artwork in the designated spots.

There are also special moldings that can be placed at the ceiling to enable art to be hung by wire or fishline on mirror, irregular stone surfaces, or where a collection will be relocated or changed often. This gives great flexibility without damaging your walls.

88. What about plants?

Plants, trees and floral arrangements are lovely and needed accessories. The object is to bring a little of the outside in. Plants add warmth and a sense of artistic beauty to a space whether they are real, petrified or artificial.

If they are real, water and feed them! If they are not maintained, their beauty is lost. If they are artificial, make sure they are good silks to enhance the décor. Live plants and trees and professional arrangements on tables, in entry ways and alongside furniture, often provide the finishing touch to complete a room.

89. How do you start to accessorize?

After the basic furniture is placed in the room, look at the wall space and empty spaces in bookcases, display cabinets and on tables. Certain areas need a focal point to unify the furniture setting.

Go shopping at home first! Are there pieces you would like to display that you've always loved or have been in the family for a long time? Do you have a hobby or interest that has made you a "collector"? Perhaps it's old trains or dolls, or pen knives or owls, or photos you've taken of your travels or posters you've collected from various museums. As long as they are presented or framed well, they make excellent accessories.

When shopping for art, go to several galleries and shops. Learn about the art form and the artist. Don't be hasty, but don't ignore the pull of a work that attracts you from the start. Art is very personal, but if you choose to become a collector, make sure you know and check the value of the pieces (independent appraisal companies are available) before you buy.

The style and the mood often affect the selection of the main accessory which will usually be the focal point of a room or a setting in the room. It is often difficult to visualize how a major accessory will look until you actually put it in the space. For this reason, certain shops allow a "take home on consignment" arrangement, where you pay in advance with the understanding that you may return what you don't like for a refund. This is the best possible approach to accessorizing if you are not retaining professional help.

90. Where do you learn how to accessorize like the professionals?

Short of hiring personal professional help, accessory shops often have trained staff to assist you. Remember, they want to sell what they have, so make sure the final decisions are yours. Look at magazines and take design books out of the library to see how the pros do it. Go to showhouses where many designers do model room settings, as well as model homes, where accessories often "sell" the houses. In short, it takes time, education and patience, but the end result is worth it because the right accessories make all the difference. Don't rush. The right piece is worth waiting or searching for, and the quest should be fun!

Chapter X

Decorating With A Budget

91. Why is it necessary to have a decorating budget?

Budgets are necessary in decorating for the same reason they are necessary in life in general. If you want to know that you have enough money to complete the project, you need to know what each item of the project costs before you begin. This includes construction or renovation costs as well. Often, that part of the project expends much more than anticipated, and too few funds are left for interior decorating. If you know in advance that you've exceeded your budget, you have an opportunity to make other choices to either balance your budget or agree to wait to complete your project when you can provide additional funds.

92. How do you know which are important budget items for you?

By making a list of the functional necessities, as well as a wish list, you can prioritize. Realistically analyze your long-term and short-term needs. For example, if you are living in a rental apartment or home, or plan to reside where you are for less than five years, costly wall-to-wall carpeting, wall coverings and custom built-ins should not be a priority. Select major items that are basic and classic, that will stand the test of time, style-wise as well as quality-wise. Fads, or what's in, will soon be "out".

Try not to compromise quality. If you can't afford to buy everything at once, think about buying less and adding more later, rather than settling for uncomfortable furniture or poor workmanship that won't wear well. If you know that the funds you allotted must complete the entire project, leave some monies for accessories so that your home will look "finished".

93. How do you set up a budget?

Set up a ledger sheet listing all the items you want and need, including a budget line for art and accessories. Start comparison shopping. Most large stores and specialty shops have sale times. Many have outlet stores where there are great "mark down" items. Look carefully for damages or mismatches, however.

Don't forget to add labor costs to your ledger sheet. Upholstery labor costs are usually separate from the fabrics you select for seating and window treatments. Wallpaper hanging and painting are separate from the actual cost of the wallpaper. Tile installation is separate from tile selection. Ask about delivery charges and other shipping fees. Don't forget to include tax.

94. When is "spending more" smarter?

If you own your own home, condo or co-op, improvements to permanent areas such as kitchens and baths can mean better resale value, as well as better living for you while you are there. Renovation or construction additions appreciate the value of your home, while making it feasible to remain there, rather than moving to larger quarters where you still need to decorate. If you don't wish to relocate, change schools, churches, neighbors, etc. this is a viable and often cost effective option, often times funded by home improvement loans or second mortgages.

95. What do you do if you have very little resources?

Paint instead of wallpaper and plan on doing it yourself, or with the help of willing and knowledgeable friends or family. Clean up and organize. Get rid of the mess and clutter and see what a difference that makes! Look for sales and bargains that are legitimate, such as end-of-year white sales, clearance center specials, wallpaper outlets, rug remnants, tag and garage sales (people don't always know what they're getting rid of!). If you are handy, go to fabric outlets and make your own slipcovers or curtains. Do-it-yourself kits are available for refinishing old furniture.

In addition, today, ready-made sheeting and matching ensembles cut the cost and create "decorator bedrooms" for a fraction of the cost of custom. Accessorize with items you already own- books, plants, collectibles-or buy posters or prints and frame them professionally, but inexpensively. Don't, however, change the floor plan. Compromising function is not necessary, and in the long run, is the least cost-effective method.

Chapter XI

Working With An Interior Designer

96. What is the function of an interior designer?

An interior designer is a professionally trained individual whose job is to assist people in need of decorating services. Their training has provided them with the skills to design floor plans and arrange furniture, provide elevational (straight-on view of one wall), axonometrical (perspective) drawings and renderings when needed. They recommend sources and assist in selections based on client's needs for flooring, wall covering, window treatments, fabrics, furniture and other trades, as well as labor to install them. In addition, the scope of their work often includes collaboration with architects and builders, plumbers, electricians and landscape designers.

97. How do interior designers work and how can they save you money?

Hourly Fee

Some work on an hourly fee. As such, this fee can vary from $50 to $200 per hour, or more, depending on the yearly income of the designer. This method takes into account, however, hours spent by staff members, which may not necessarily be billed at the same fee. Such a method includes an itemization of billable extras, such as phone time, travel expenses, printing costs, etc. Other professionals paid by hourly fees are accountants and attorneys. Hourly wages are not related to product sold. The contract with your designer should state that all products purchased will be at designer's wholesale prices, if that is your agreement, passing on to you the benefit of all guarantees and warranties, as well as a sizable discount off retail cost.

Cost Plus Percentage

Another payment method is one of cost plus percentage. For example, the showroom retail price of a sofa is $1,000. The designer's cost at 40% discount is $600. At a billable charge of 25% of designer's cost, the sofa would cost $750. (25% of $600, or $150 plus original $600 cost). This would represent a savings to the client of $250 off retail, a well as providing expertise and a wider range of sources from which to purchase.

Flat Fee

A third payment method which designers often use is a flat fee structure. This method is based on estimating time spent on a project, as well as rough cost estimates. The flat fee generally drops slightly as the magnitude of the job increases, provided it's done in one phase. For example, a project whose wholesale rough cost estimate might be $10,000 would generate a designer cost fee of $2,000, if done at once. It might generate a cost fee of $2,500 to $3,000 if done in two or more stages.

Flat fee arrangements are equitable to both client and design professionals in that payment is based on time spent and services rendered, not married to any fixed item. For example, if a sofa costs $1,000 or $5,000, on a flat fee arrangement, you would pay the same. On a cost plus percentage arrangement, you would pay five times more in designer's fees for the more expensive sofa.

Square Foot Method

A square foot method is sometimes used by commercial as well as residential interior designers. They multiply the square footage of a space by a pre-determined dollar amount. Space planning services are billed in this manner.

Retail Cost

Retail cost is a charging method that has fallen into disuse because it is difficult to apply to the labor and supervision aspects of a project. Trained professionals also resent having to "hide" their fees in retail costs. They prefer to have clients know how much their skills and services cost.

Whatever method is used, a consultation fee is generally separate. This fee is for an initial and exploratory survey, including floor plans and furniture arrangements, presentation boards, and a budget estimate. In some cases, elevational drawings and renderings are also included. This is generally charged out as a separate flat fee. A consultation phase is beneficial to the client because they can then have all the information they need to make an intelligent decision before they proceed.

Often a retainer is required which is applied to future design fees. In each method, however, the client is still paying less than retail. But paying less than retail should not be the only reason to work with a designer. Doing anything yourself will take lots of time, taste and the expertise to plan, visualize and coordinate sources. Competent professionals can make it look easy - but anyone who has tried it knows better!

98. Do you give up control and relinquish your right to choose what you want when you work with an interior designer?

Most people fear that an interior designer will take over and design a project that is not of their choosing. In truth, that is up to the client. Some hire designers whose distinctive style is what they are looking for (ie: Mario Buatta, for his English chintzy prints). They might give them the key to their residence and go off to vacation in Europe for the duration of the project.

Most people, however, want to be a part of the selection process, and opt to remain present, as well as on site during the actual installation. The professional designer can and should provide what is needed for both types of clients. The first type of client requires a competent and professional reproduction of a style the designer has popularized. The second requires an understanding of the client's wants and needs, as well as their lifestyle, color preference and budget constraints. Through careful questioning and mutual dialogue, the designer can elicit this information. The designer uses visual aids such as scale floor plans and furniture arrangements, fabric presentation boards and renderings, to help the client "see" the space. A budget analysis prior to the placement of orders will detail the cost of the project as well.

These standard procedures amongst professionals in the design field allow for a variety of choices on the part of the client, as well as an understanding of the costs. In truth, it is the client who decides how much input is comfortable for them. Once this is agreed upon with their designer, there is usually no problem.

If a person wishes to "go it alone" after the initial presentation is made, many designers will sign a release or agreement to that effect and are then compensated for their work. Most clients, however, after they have approved the design concept, color schemes and budget choose the security of working with a professional through co-ordination and completion, particularly when an important part of the design project is accessorizing.

The true art and skill of a fine professional designer is in educating and developing the client's own best taste and then providing an environment in which they can live and work comfortably, beautifully and happily.

99. What should you expect from your interior designer?

Your designer should have the skills to provide you with all the services you require. Ask about their credentials, check references, view examples of their work, visit their office and shop and most of all, see if your personalities are compatible. If you have a particular design style in mind, discuss this and determine how the designer would approach it for your dwelling and lifestyle. Your designer should also present you with a contract detailing the scope of their work and the fee to do it, as well as an approximate time frame for completion. Before beginning a project, all of these items should be provided and approved.

100. What should your interior designer expect from you?

The ideal client is one who is honest and open about their wants, needs and budget. They ask questions when they don't understand or can't visualize a presentation, which enables the designer to know when the client is unsure. They make clear what they don't like, even if they are not always positive about the final choice, and they keep an open mind when designers present new ideas, styles or solutions.

Designers are most happy working with people who are realistic about time frame, pay promptly on request and offer positive reaction to ongoing work and final completion. They appreciate being enlightened about a problem in a manner that encourages a solution. In short, they desire a positive relationship that will continue for years after the design project is successfully completed, for their reputation and future business depends on it and their need for artistic fruition can be satisfied in no other way.